PIANO · VOCAL · GUITAR

TOP HITS OF 2005

ISBN 1-4234-0144-1

HAL•LEONARD®
CORPORATION

7777 W. BLUEMOUND RD. P.O. BOX 13819 MILWAUKEE, WI 53213

Visit Hal Leonard Online at
www.halleonard.com

AMERICAN BABY

Words and Music by MARK BATSON,
DAVID J. MATTHEWS, BOYD TINSLEY,
LEROI MOORE, CARTER BEAUFORD
and STEFAN LESSARD

To Coda

will. I _____ see you _____ in _____ life

D.S. al Coda

hope I _____ don't get _____ left be - hind.

CODA

| Bm | A | Gmaj9 | Bm | A |

I hope you _____ stay, _____ beau - ti - ful

| Gmaj9 | Bm | A |

ba - by. I _____ hope you _____

BEAUTIFUL SOUL

Words and Music by ANDY DODD
and ADAM WATTS

BLESS THE BROKEN ROAD

Words and Music by MARCUS HUMMON,
BOBBY BOYD and JEFF HANNA

D.S. al Coda

GIRL

Words and Music by BEYONCE KNOWLES, KELLY ROWLAND,
EDDIE ROBINSON, DON DAVIS,
ANGELA BEYINCE, SEAN GARRETT,
MICHELLE WILLIAMS and PATRICK DOUTHIT

Take a min-ute, girl, ___ come sit down, ___ and
See, what y'all ___ don't know a-bout him, ___ is I

girl, _____ you're my girl, __ we're your girls. _ We want you to know that we love you.

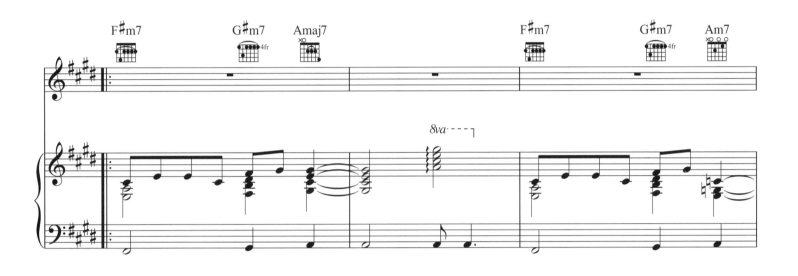

Repeat and Fade | **Optional Ending**

GIVE A LITTLE BIT

Words and Music by RICK DAVIES
and ROGER HODGSON

KARMA

Words and Music by KERRY BROTHERS, JR.,
ALICIA KEYS and TANEISHA SMITH

Moderately slow

Weren't you ___ the one ___ that said ___ that you ___ don't want ___ me an - y - more, ___
And when ___ you came ___ home you'd ___ al - ways ___ have some ___ sor - ry ___ ex - cuse, ___

down.) Now ___ who's cry - in,' ___ de - sir - in' ___ to come back ___ to me? ___

HOME

Words and Music by AMY FOSTER-GILLIES,
MICHAEL BUBLÉ and ALAN CHANG

Moderately slow

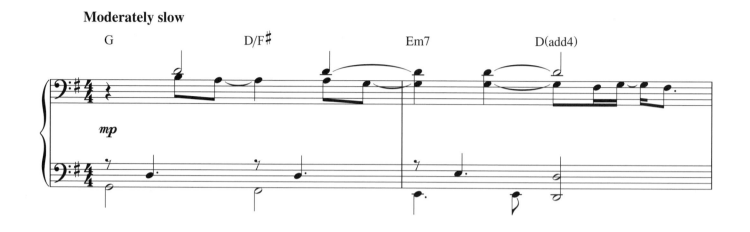

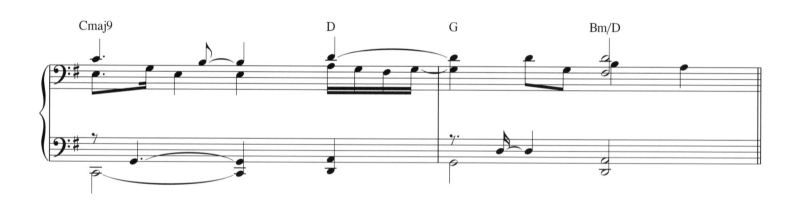

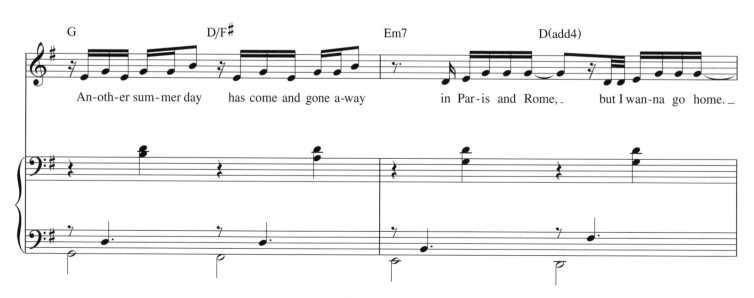

An-oth-er sum-mer day has come and gone a-way in Par-is and Rome, but I wan-na go home.

INCOMPLETE

Words and Music by LINDY ROBBINS,
DAN MUCKALA and JESS CATES

*Recorded a half step lower.

LET ME GO

Words and Music by BRAD ARNOLD,
ROBERT HARRELL, CHRISTOPHER HENDERSON
and MATTHEW ROBERTS

Moderate Rock

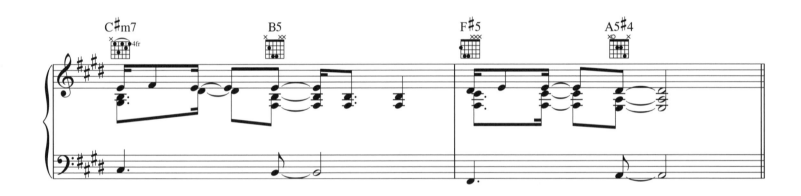

One __ more kiss __ could be __ the best __ thing.
I dream a - head __ to what __ I hope __ for.

LIVE LIKE YOU WERE DYING

Words and Music by CRAIG WISEMAN
and TIM J. NICHOLS

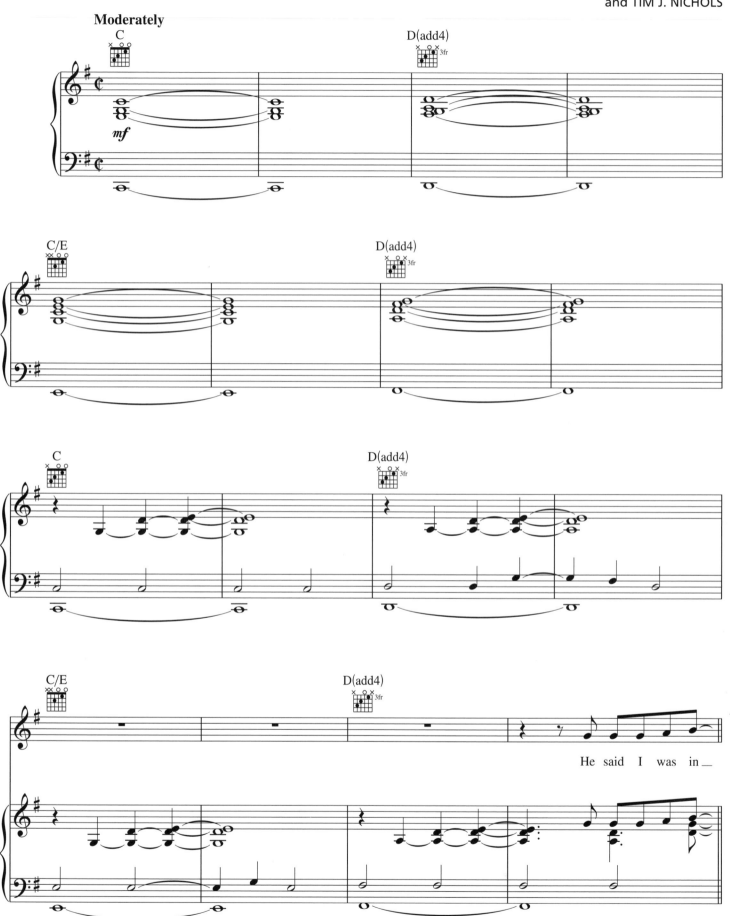

He said I was in __

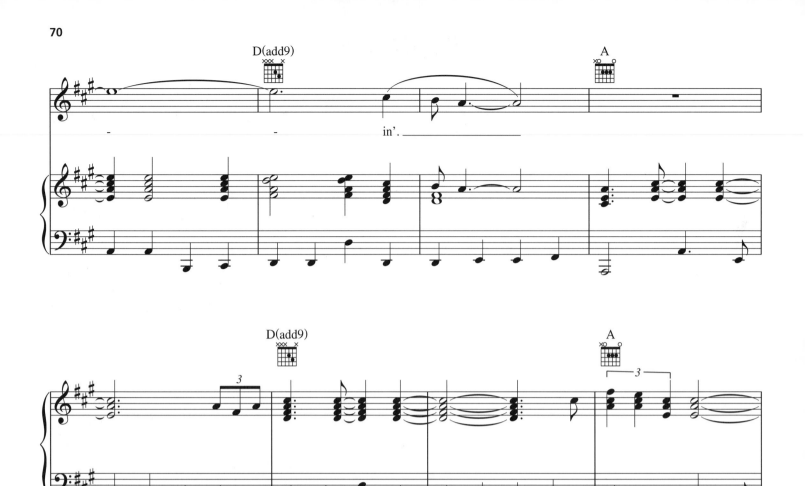

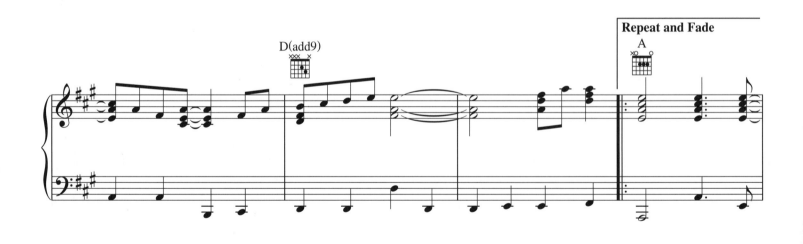

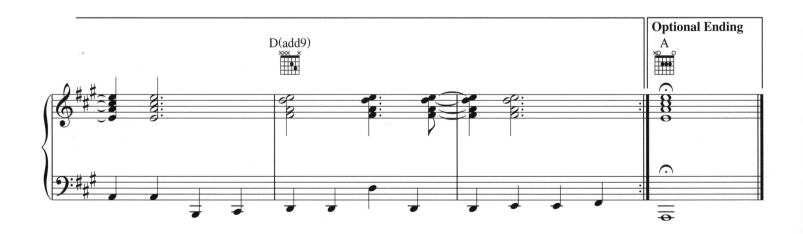

LONELY

Words and Music by ALIAUNE THIAM,
BOBBY VINTON and GENE ALLEN

Lone - ly,
lone - ly, } I'm Mis - ter Lone - ly. I have no -

bod - y for __ my o _____ own. __ I'm __ so

lone - ly.

LONELY NO MORE

Words and Music by
ROB THOMAS

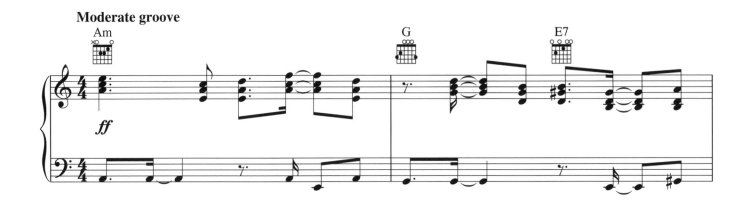

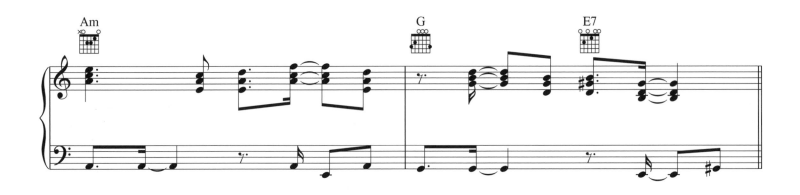

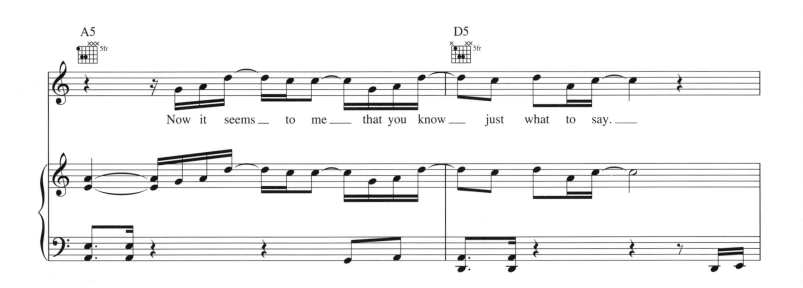

Now it seems__ to me__ that you know__ just what to say.__

SPEED OF SOUND

Words and Music by GUY BERRYMAN,
WILL CHAMPION, CHRIS MARTIN
and JON BUCKLAND

MR. BRIGHTSIDE

Words and Music by BRANDON FLOWERS,
DAVE KEUNING, MARK STOERMER
and RONNIE VANNUCCI

*Recorded a half step lower.

Bright - side.

OH

Words and Music by CHRISTOPHER BRIDGES,
ANDRE HARRIS, VIDAL DAVIS
and CIARA HARRIS

D.S. al Coda

Light skinned big chicks, fel-las call 'em red-bones. Close cuts, braids long, gang-stas love 'em all. __

CODA

low, __ oh. __ Rap: (See additional lyrics)

Play 3 times

Oh, __ 'round here we rid-in'

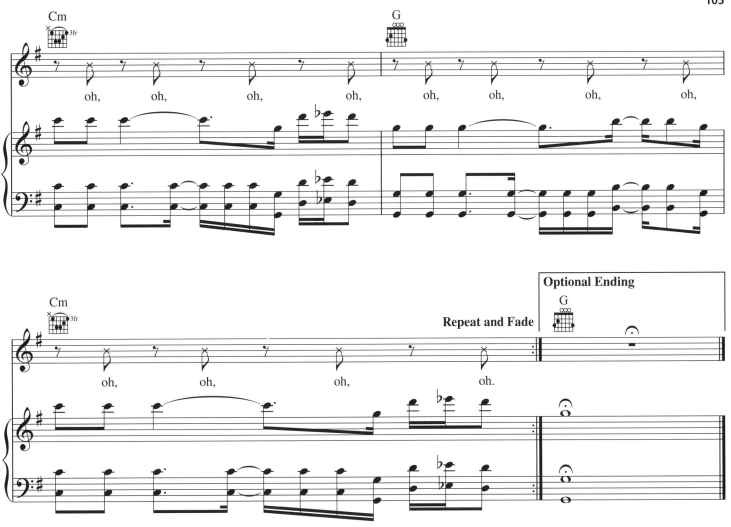

Additional Lyrics

Southern style, get wild. Old school's comin' down in a diff'rent color whip, whip, whip.
Picture perfect, you might wanna take a flick, flick, flick, flick, flick.
Call up Jazzey, tell him pop the bottles 'cause we got another hit, hit, hit.
Wanna go plat'num, I'm who you should get, get, get, get, get.
Ludacrais on the track. Get back. Trick switch on the lac I'm flexin' steel.
Same price ev'ry time. Hot song, jumped on 'cause Ciara got sex appeal.
And I keep the meanest, cleanest, baddest, spinnin' on stainless wheels.
Could care less about your genius. I bump your status. I keep the stainless steel.
Trunk rattlin', what's happenin' huh? I don't even think I need to speed.
Bass travelin', face cracklin' huh? Turn it up and make the speakers bleed.
Dirty south, we ballin' dog. And never think about fallin' dog.
Ghetto harmonizin', surprisin', run it back 'cause the song is called.

SINCE U BEEN GONE

Words and Music by MARTIN SANDBERG
and LUKASZ GOTTWALD

Moderately fast

Here's the thing: we
You ded - i - cat - ed, you
How can I put it? You

start - ed out friends. It was cool, but it was all pre-tend. ____
took the ___ time. Was-n't long ___ 'til I called you mine. ____
put me ___ on. I e - ven fell ___ for that stu - pid love ___ song.)

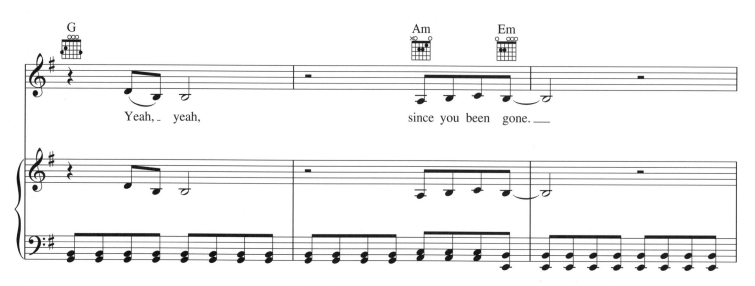

Yeah, ___ yeah, since you been gone. ____

SOMEWHERE ONLY WE KNOW

Words and Music by TIM RICE-OXLEY,
RICHARD HUGHES and TOM CHAPLIN

SUNDAY MORNING

Words and Music by ADAM LEVINE
and JESSE CARMICHAEL

D.S. al Coda

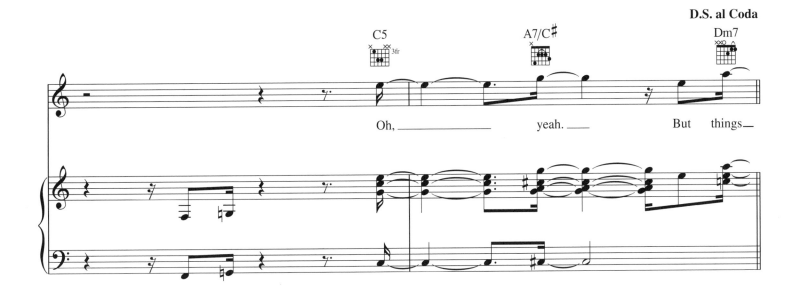

Oh, _____ yeah. ____ But things_

- ing. Driv - in' slow, _____ yeah, __ yeah. __ Ahh, yeah, _ yeah. __ Ahh, all __

124

TRUTH IS

Words and Music by CARSTEN SCHACK, KENNETH KARLIN, ERNIE ISLEY,
O'KELLY ISLEY, RONALD ISLEY, RUDOLPH ISLEY,
MARVIN ISLEY, CHRISTOPHER JASPER, THABISO NKHEREANYE,
PATRICK SMITH and ALEXANDER CANTRALL

Recorded a half step higher.

He was a fam-il-iar face__ from a chap-ter in__ my past.__

Talked for a while, asked him how he's been. __ Said that he was see-in' some-bod-y and __

__ told me this was gon-na last,__ show-in' me her pho-to-graph.__

And all the feel-in's that I thought were gone ____

129

TRUE

Words and Music by RYAN CABRERA,
JIMMY HARRY and SHEPPARD SOLOMON

Recorded a half step lower.

WE BELONG TOGETHER

Words and Music by MARIAH CAREY,
JERMAINE DUPRI, MANUEL SEAL,
JOHNTA AUSTIN, DARNELL BRISTOL,
KENNETH EDMONDS, SIDNEY JOHNSON,
PATRICK MOTEN, BOBBY WOMACK
and SANDRA SULLY